Tense & Still

Also by Carolyn Cordon

My Dog, Eleanor Curtain Publishing 2004
Dig It! Gardening Tips for Dogs, self-published 2007
damaged children Precious Gems, Gary MacRae 2011
Mick, Jane and Me – Living well with MS, self-published 2013
Doggone It – Mindfulness from a Dog's Point of View,
self-published 2016

Carolyn Cordon

Tense & Still

Tense & Still
ISBN 978 1 76041 207 4
Copyright © text Carolyn Cordon 2016
Cover photo © okeanaslt

First published 2016 by
GINNINDERRA PRESS
PO Box 3461 Port Adelaide 5015
www.ginninderrapress.com.au

Contents

Dogs & Cats	7
Ananka's pantoum	9
Pets/Pests	10
A Jillaroo's Lament	11
What is a Dog?	12
Looking for trouble	13
Instinct	14
Walled Garden	15
Rusty Thoughts	16
Painful Lesson	17
Out damned cat	18
No Mousers Here…	19
Beijing Thirty Years Ago	20
Establishing a Persona	21
Short Poems and Haiku	22
Birds	23
Judgement	25
Birdies Tweet	26
What is Memory?	27
Strategic Air Offensive	28
Life's Connections	29
Springtime in black & white	30
Revelations	31
Gentle Thoughts	32
At Conversations Café	33
Still Safe	35
Price is paid	36
Hidden truths	37
Interpretation	38

Starlings	39
Not Alone	40
Short Poems and Haiku	41

Other Critters — 43

Rabbits aren't my kind of pet…	45
I'm sort of sorry	46
Not all hit and run victims are statistically noted…	47
The End	48
Road to death and distraction	49
Hit and Run	50
Why Did the Snake Cross the Road?	51
A salty tale	52
Whatever it takes	53
Attacked!	54
A long way to go	55
Never Again	56
Man versus Nature	57
A lesson learnt	58
Spider thoughts	59
Eight Legs	60
Goodbye, Spidey	61
Short Poems and Haiku	63

Dogs & Cats

Ananka's pantoum

Crouched down low, tense and still
waiting for the perfect time.
She'll wait there silently until
that perfect moment, so sublime.

Waiting for the perfect time
to launch herself into the air –
that perfect moment so sublime;
delicious tension, studied stare.

To launch herself into the air –
with birds about she's never bored;
delicious tension, studied stare
then the leap that brings reward.

With birds about she's never bored,
study, watch, listen, learn,
then the leap that brings reward.
Nothing's free, you have to earn.

Study, watch, listen, learn,
apply the knowledge in her head.
Nothing's free, you have to earn
that little birdie now so dead.

And so it goes on every day –
she'll wait there silently until
every bird has gone away;
crouched down low, tense and still

Pets/Pests

A handy trick,
for a hound that's quick
is killing venomous snakes.

But hounds that are slow,
don't you know,
are likely seen as fakes.

My hounds know the way
on a sunny day,
to dispatch a wriggling pest.

Snakes shouldn't roam,
near our home –
I'm thinking that would be best.

For snakes that die,
I seldom cry,
though it pains me a little bit.

And if you're taking bets
on my choice of pets
dogs win, I have to admit!

A Jillaroo's Lament

These past few nights I've settled down
my head between my knees,
and cuddled close my kelpie dog
although he makes me sneeze.

My only friend, he stays close by,
ignores my sneezy noise
as I lament, with weepy eyes
my bad luck with the boys.

My kelpie dog, Red Ned's his name,
he tells me with his eyes,
'Forget the guys, they're never true,
they'll only tell you lies.'

'I know,' I say, and stroke his chin,
'and Ned, I'll tell you true,
the blokes I chase don't measure up
half as good as you!'

Neddy smiles his kelpie smile
and nods his wise old head.
And people, let me tell you now –
he keeps me warm in bed!

What is a Dog?

A friend
An ally
A reason to get out of bed

A walk buddy
An asset
But the source of those hairs been shed.

A dog is all of these and more
A dog can be different things, for sure
But a dog is a treasure and source of pleasure,
For without a dog, what fun is leisure?

Looking for trouble

The snake was there on the lawn
dead or dying, head chopped off
tail still a-twitch,
the dogs, hunting instincts alive,
baying for more blood.

Inside again, we all calm down
and think on what's occurred…
then valiant hunter collapses and we face
the possibility of the winner
losing her life.

Emergency phone call,
rushed trip to possible salvation –
our son become man
carries then lays her down on the table
before our chosen ones.

Treatment given, questions answered,
Missy left overnight
with more treatment, but no guarantees.
Next day, happy girl home again
out looking for trouble once more…

Instinct

Prey flies past, the hunt begins,
hound's senses all switched on.
Born to chase, not hunt through bins,
in the moment, tameness gone.

He pounces down, grasps it tight
shakes it to break its neck.
It doesn't move, its end in sight,
the bloodied snake a wreck…

Walled Garden

Safe and secure behind the high wall
with garden tended by another
and a lawn you'll never have to mow yourself.

You've friends and facilities galore, pleasant walks,
swimming, gym and bowls to use or not –
the decision yours, no worries, no stress.

Who wouldn't want to live like this? Life
stripped back for convenience, and pressure-free,
with Deb in charge in the office, it's all going well.

I envy you a little, Mum, with your peaceful Gardens life,
but I know with my noisy bounding hounds,
it's not the place for me and mine.

Because I like tall dogs and even taller trees,
winds that rush past, unrestrained by bricks
and I love my far horizons…

Rusty Thoughts

He's still doing a long sit-stay,
minding the way to our front door.
Rusty's a good dog, never barks
or whines and only strays when
and where the wind takes him
and he never goes very far.

We found him on a road trip, halfway
across Australia – he was in a shop
we stopped at, like he was waiting for us;
driving off, we said we'd buy him
if we stopped, if he was still there
and if we had any money left going home.

He was, and we did, so into
the back of the car he went.
Rusty's settled in real well at home,
in his spot near the front door, next to
the donkey with two pots of flowers
on its back, just under the front veranda –

two life-sized metal mates,
craft works turned to art,
in the shape of a poem.

Painful Lesson

Broken bones? Who can tell
without X-ray's truth.
But pain is there
when foot is touched
so I leave it alone.

It's a silly tale
of a silly hound
who leapt without looking
leaving me
to pay the price –

blood and bruising a painful reminder
to keep out of the kitchen
when the beasts are feeding…
or to put on
my bloody shoes!

Out damned cat

It slinks around the front of our place,
black cat with white highlights
taunting our dogs from its safe spot
on the other side of the fence.

Dogs bark and bark hysterically
and if neighbours don't like the noise,
bad luck chaps, we don't like your cat
that trespasses here, repeatedly.

Our dogs bark, their cat wanders –
Nature's creatures tamed by man
trying to find a way to exist –
animals and humans, living together.

Their wild pasts haunt them –
Nature and nurture wrestling,
battling with wild creatures,
prey to cat, dog and man – the losers…

No Mousers Here…

Our dogs are sofa dogs,
pampered pooches
living luxurious
and lazy
Western lives,
hunting only
for the best sofa spot
while mice and men
reign in the kitchen.

Quite different are Soviet cats,
working hard
for the state
the way good cats do
and other feline hunters,
catching, then presenting,
the evidence,
satisfying instincts
and owners.

Beijing Thirty Years Ago

A stranger to their country,
I still knew the end in sight
for the black and white cat
perched atop the tiny house
down that rough little street.

Sitting just higher than head height
cat looked down at the crowd
waiting for it, lidded carry basket
at the ready. Watching, I recalled
Chinese food jokes about cat.

They seemed to be calling it
but the cat wouldn't budge.
Then our bus moved on again
leaving us Westerners pondering
cultural differences and cats…

Establishing a Persona

Cat is a symbol
I decline to embrace
Cat scratch tainted my flesh
At an early age
Friendship spurned by puss
As I now spurn feline charms
Scat, cat!
I don't want one such as you
Twisting and twining around me
Planning to bring me down –
Return to Satan's sanctuary
And leave me alone…

Short Poems and Haiku

puppy
playful, cute
bites, races, jumps
full-speed little dynamo
tornado!

three pups
fast asleep in a pile –
nearly lunchtime

nursing home visit –
the son remembers his father
kicking their old dog

Birds

Judgement

A chicken
A road
Is there merit
in being
on the other side?
And who are we
to judge
what chicken does
        anyway?

Birdies Tweet

When I hear the birdies tweet
I sometimes think it'd be neat
to fly up with them in the trees –
what silly thoughts, though, are these?

Birds are birds but I'm a person –
too big to fly, of that I'm certain!
I'll stay down here and watch them fly,
keep to the ground, not fly up high.

Or maybe I'll take a glider ride,
or hot-air balloon, with birds I'll glide!
These are the only ways, it seems
I can meet my flying dreams!

What is Memory?

Memory is a twittering bird
flying here and there
telling tales, then winging away,
into sky's blue vastness,
leaving secrets concealed.

Memory is an overstuffed turkey,
roasted to perfection,
pleasure in every bite,
or underdone pink flesh bleeding,
meaning flowing away from fork.

Memory is a wise owl
that suddenly appears
in headlight glare
to snatch up prey, then swoops off,
to savour its catch in dead of night.

Strategic Air Offensive

Zit zit zit, they cry
as they bomb
through the garden
blasting my silence.

Shrapnel of sound hits
as I sit, stunned
at the explosion
of colour.

One two three lorikeets
strafing my solitude.
Mission accomplished
they return to base.

Life's Connections

I accepted the request happily enough –
'Could I put food scraps in the compost bin?'
my husband asks me one winter day.
'Of course I could, thrilled to help,'
I say. I love us making our own compost,
making good things instead of land fill.
So into the kitchen, gather scraps,
then, 'Come on, dogs, let's go!'

Outside, next to the pool, where bin is,
I marvel at cool, clear water and birds
which zoom down from wide blue sky
then drop down to water, going about
their day's work, ignoring me
but watching out for the dogs.
Scraps in, lid back on, then tumble
scraps together, compost on its way.

I examine feeble growth on nearest rose,
smell yellow blooms on bush next to it,
then I dead head the third and oldest one.
In this leaf-denuded largest bush,
a handful-sized nest, empty of life,
but filled with interest in its making up –
blue thread, dog hair, my own hair
all went together to make this tiny home.

An autumn miracle,
to fill me with wonder.

Springtime in black & white

There's a willy wagtail
picking officiously through
piles of wind-blown treasure,
searching for nesting material
in readiness for things to come.
I sit at the dining table
and watch him/her,
thinking on my own nest –
warm and safe
and sheltering us all.
The bird finds the perfect twig
and flies away, while I
put dirty dishes in the sink
my 'lazy' tendencies
redeemed…

Revelations

In the ordinary,
is the extraordinary –
open your eyes
and your mind
and it will be revealed to you.

First gum tree seen after a trip abroad
intense drying heat of the northerly winds in summer
pigeons always knowing the way home
seeds growing from tiny to huge
A person, even knowing death is inevitable
still reaching for immortality…

Gentle Thoughts

On the road from home to Mallala,
travelling to watch the men of the house
compete and win, I hope –
my thoughts wander from lawn bowls
to the road ahead and tomorrow,
and tomorrow's road, all winding
their gentle way around my head.
Those thoughts are wrenched
from me by a bird, up there in the sky –
hovering over the paddock I'm passing.
What bird is that? It's a bird of prey
I know that much, but which?
I rapidly go through the possibilities
lamenting my lack of resources
in my car, when my home library
would show me the truth…
Will not knowing which bird it was
prey on my thoughts, I wonder
when I'm watching the game?
Only time will tell…

At Conversations Café

Eavesdropping
on galahs, or more likely
it's those corellas

plotting who to torment next.
Bunyip's editor
gets letters

complaining
about corellas'
rapacious avian ways –

'They're destroying trees,' they say.
But the trees still grow.
They're pruning

them, that's what
I think. Pruning them
so the trees regenerate.

New leaves, new twigs, new branches.
Corellas challenge
gum trees' growth.

Challenges
help these trees to grow
ever stronger, these years on.

But what can I say? It's not
my town, Gawler, and
not my sleep

being wrecked.
So I keep my thoughts
to myself, and watch – trees, birds…

Still Safe

Territory invaded
they swoop
again
and again
protecting
their home.

Cyclist ducks
wobbles
rides on
thankful
the magpie
missed again.

Price is paid

Road claims another victim
I see it as I drive past –
black and white, forever still
the unnamed, unknown corpse
a magpie, my first thought,
yet another one.

But driving past again
I see elegant long neck stretched
as though reaching out
as though asking
for acknowledgement.

A waterbird, stranger
to the usually dry plains
where I live, where rain
has come, but the river
is yet to run.

I acknowledge you, cormorant
you were here and I mourn you –
a stranger who paid the price
for being in the wrong place
at the wrong time…

Hidden truths

Clothes and branches wave gently
in mild autumn breeze
and the big blue sky has opened up
to let the sunshine in.
Turtledoves and other birds
provide a changing chorus –
ah yes, my life seems grand!

Then two honeyeaters crash
into both my thoughts
and my son's window, adjacent
to my outdoor seat, bringing reality
back to my loose and dreamy thoughts.
Honeyeaters shuffle their feathers and fly off –
all of us shaken by hidden things…

Interpretation

Why is it
that whenever
I see
or hear
birds mating,
it looks
and sounds
like rape?

Starlings

The dead gum tree
shed its leaves
many seasons back,
but branches still reach out
to the sun, with buds as black
as death, until buds flower
into dark flight
at human approach,
showing life
of a different kind.

Not Alone

Breeze plays with chimes
willie wagtail sings along
cheeping and chirping in tune.
Wind through pine trees
a constant droning backdrop
sparrows join in too
their repetitive chirps
a reminder I am not alone…

Short Poems and Haiku

a gentle spring breeze –
front yard shared with birds
and motorbike roar

cricket season –
seagulls and people all flock
to Adelaide Oval

hanging out washing –
sparrow near me holds a strand
of blue in her beak

nearly summer –
ibis litter the paddock
along Highway One

wind chimes –
galahs tumbling
through the sky

three magpies
stand over the injured starling –
pecking order

at the pond
waiting for goldfish to appear –
a wattlebird calls

lorikeet's call
answered by many –
gum blossom

the magpie
leaves road kill as I pass –
open road

rainless clouds –
air force choppers and two kites
all circling

gum's limp leaves –
pigeon slowly lifts one wing
then the other

springtime puddle –
crested pigeon and its reflection
both strutting

two doves balance
on the power line above –
clouds drift by

Other Critters

Rabbits aren't my kind of pet...

As a household pet?
I'm not so sure –
you can cuddle them,
but I want more.

I want affection
with intelligent eyes,
not a fluffy critter
with edible thighs.

So keep your bunny
if you must have one
but a puppy dog
is lots more fun!

I'm sort of sorry

What do you do, when the vermin just sits there
a long-eared bit of fluff, with a cute little tail,
on the unforgiving road, with nowhere to go?
It sat there, as I thought on it at super speed
and drove over it, crushing my heart
as well as the rabbit, but thinking of crops,
pests, the past and the future. It's still there,
traffic-flattened, cuteness completely lost –
with crops not yet planted, but made safe
from this particular bunny rabbit...

Not all hit and run victims are statistically noted…

Passing by the death scene –
vermin for sure, but rabbit or hare?
The extended ear rising above
blood-spattered body hinted at hare –
but I wasn't sure which

and the crow in attendance
probably didn't care.
It took a careful step back
as I drove by, watching me
but keeping an eye on its dinner…

The End

Fox corpses haunt me as I drive by –
they've crossed the road, paddock
to paddock, with ill intent.
Their plushly furred still bodies
accuse me and my car, although
their deaths came before
this journey today even began.

Foxes, not native to this place
as their prey, too, is not native –
both species brought here many years ago –
sheep to feed all of the people,
foxes to provide sport for a chosen few,
with fences to keep one lot in,
but not the other lot out.

Farmers lament losses and count costs
but lambs pay the ultimate price,
as their defiler does too, sometimes.
Fox and lamb harking back,
to cooler climes, where the hunt
and farming this way came into being –
death will always end the struggle.

Road to death and distraction

I saw it there
on my way to the shop

the kangaroo
who'd hopped its last hop

lying roadside, bashed
and battered

a car crash victim
nothing more mattered

the animal's dead
my heart crying

who else mourns
this creature's dying?

Hit and Run

Warm road seduces them
one side of road to the other –
reptiles, four legs or none
who knows why they went?

But their crossing days are over –
hit and run drivers
have hit
and run…

Why Did the Snake Cross the Road?

Was it there as a warning
or just a sign of season's change?
Whatever the reason,
the creature pounded my heart,
bang, bang, bang
as the shiny undulating
metre and a half of it
disappeared
into the grass
on the left side,
the sinister side,
of the road.
I did you farewell, snake,
may we never, ever
meet again…

A salty tale

Oh silly frog, what have you done?
The swimming pool is not for you…
It's sparkly and clear and looks like fun,
I agree, it is, that's certainly true.

But the water there is toxic to frogs
I've seen what happens, it's bad
It's fine for people, or even for dogs
but what happens to frogs makes me so sad.

And of frogs, I admit I've become quite fond
with their questioning eyes and mournful croak
but transferring them from pool to pond
is slowly becoming less than a joke.

I wish they'd accept they really oughta
think of their safety and think of me,
and only swim in pond's safe water –
our swimming pool's nearly as salt as the sea!

Whatever it takes

Kelly lets flies in to share her day,
the blowies drive her husband nuts –
John arms himself with insect spray
and blasts flies into oblivion.

'How do they get in?' he asks
but Kelly shrugs, says nothing,
not mourning her dead visitors
or caring much, there's plenty more outside.

They're just a little company to help her
get through dull days, and driving John nuts
isn't the reason why she does it,
it's just her wifely bonus…

Attacked!

The mosquito hadn't heard, obviously
that if you take the med I take
the pesky buggers
would leave you alone.
Gilenya helps well with my MS
and I was even gladder
when I read the mozzie thing,
but at the poetry reading tonight,
listening to fine words read well
and with passion,
I see the mosquito fly in front of me
then stop, settle comfortably down
not to listen to a poem or two
but to do its vampire act,
attack me and suck my blood!

A long way to go

To the millipede
I found in my house,
I say sorry

It would have been easy
to take you outside
and set you free

Instead I flushed
you away
in the kitchen sink

I know this
won't take away
what I did

But I apologise –
you did not deserve
such an ending

It seems there's still a long way
to go, on my path
to enlightenment

Never Again

I ate an insect recently,
it flew between my teeth.
I waved a hand as it came close,
but it zipped in underneath.

I tried to spit the insect out
but couldn't, I confess,
I spat and snorted – unladylike,
and created quite a mess

I nearly got the insect out
as it entered the back of my nose
but it turned around and headed along
the initial route it chose

Feeling that thing in my mouth
made me feel quite queasy,
but what to do? I swallowed
and it went down quick and easy!

It tickled my throat as it disappeared –
Never again! I thought,
my mouth shall be a bug-free zone
exactly as it ought!

Man versus Nature

I heard of a 'cat fight', witnessed by many –
my friend tried in vain not to look.
I heard of a robbery in a quiet country town
and ached at innocence lost.

Then I watched a black beetle tip over and over
struggling and winning to get back to its feet.
I wonder at it these things, and marvel anew –
Nature will win, every time.

A lesson learnt

The little boy pulls down his pants
with no regard for decency
or any good reason, I can see;
he aims a stream at toiling ants.

Panic disrupts the ordered dance
and causes much unbridled glee
at such confusion caused by pee.
But one small ant sees a chance,

it latches on to one small toe.
Giggles then rise high to screams.
Boy shakes his foot to make it go,
ending all his urine schemes
of treating insects thus, and so
a needed lesson's learnt, it seems.

Spider thoughts

Do spiders bleed?
Do their hearts ache red
for love's sad lack?

We may fear them,
but should we also mourn them
with their dark and violent deaths…

My heart aches for them
with painful red twinges of guilt –
but they will never know…

Eight Legs

Curled up high, a black blob on the wall
above the clock, its home a hole
in the woodwork.
The spider does its spidery things
coming out from time to time
but never travelling far
at least not when we're watching.
Does it go out at night, I wonder,
when we're in bed,
are there webs around the ceiling
that we don't see, capturing
tiny creatures we didn't know were there?
It's not harming us, way up there
with its eight legs carrying it
all around the walls,
while we stay down here,
all of us keeping safe and sound…

Goodbye, Spidey

Living in the wall,
on the wall,
or off and wandering,
it was with us
for several weeks.

Big and black –
a silent presence.
I called it Spidey,
and wondered
why it was there.

Then, on Good Friday
if hung from the ceiling,
on a single silken strand
seven legs curled up
one holding on tight.

There for days
unmoving, non-threatening
but constantly
present and dangling…
Was it alive?

On Easter Sunday Spidey fell,
plunging from up
near the ceiling
down, down, down
to the floor, dead.

I miss you, Spidey,
your hole in the wall
near the clock, reminds me
that life and death
don't wait…

Short Poems and Haiku

Veranda Thoughts

slug slowly
slithers southward,
its silver smear
stays…

bearded dragon on road
suddenly transforms –
gum tree bark

paddock fence
is hung with fox pelts –
frolicking lambs

new water lily –
the goldfish swim
straight past it

frost-tipped grass –
the new foal kicks
his heels up

www.ingramcontent.com/pod-product-compliance
Lightning Source LLC
Chambersburg PA
CBHW062201100526
44589CB00014B/1900